Bits of Thirst

Bits of Thirst

& other poems & translations

Jack Marshall

Blue Wind Press : Berkeley : 1976

Some of these poems
have appeared in the following magazines:
Clear Creek; American Poetry Review; Ploughshares; Suction;
Search for Tomorrow; Kayak; Toothpaste; The Iowa State Liquor Store;
Kamadhenu; Skywriting; Equal-Time; The Lamp in the Spine;
Poetry Now; The North American Review; Stooge; Delirium;
Big Moon; and Surviving in America.

Cedar Creek Press previously published some of these poems
as 'Bits of Thirst' and the long-poem 'Floats.' The author
wishes to thank editors Sam Hamod and John Henry
for permission to reprint those poems in this collection.

LIBRARY OF CONGRESS
CATALOGING IN PUBLICATION DATA:

Marshall, Jack, 1937—
Bits of thirst.

I. Title.

PS3563.A722B5   811'.5'4   75-9874
ISBN 0-912652-15-2 pbk.

designed by George Mattingly.
Cover painting by the author / Photo by Marie Bustard
printed by Braun-Brumfield, Inc.

Blue Wind Press books are available direct (820 Miramar,
Berkeley, California 94707); or through:
Bookpeople; RPM; or The Distributors.

Contents

Floats & other poems

for,
among others,
David Ian Sky Marshall

in your shoes

Wherever you imagine yourself most real,
go there.
        Out of a love that is not gentle
as the dust of a room,
but a love that happens in a room
and becomes dust,
whatever room you wake in now
is the room of your birth.

In the sleep that you are,
in the waking that you want,
you wonder how to open the windows
of your life that has come to resemble
a heaven smelling of burning angels,
where love lives but not in one place.
It migrates off the coast, heavy and spewing
like whales rising, immense, then diving
out of sight. The waterspouts are late,
but you are feeling lucky that the sky is
shaped like today over a country that flies
no flag but a few orange and blue jerseys,
the letters muddied but not torn,
the numbers, bold and blowsy
against the vacant stands.

When you smile, how the seats fill up
with a cheer!—like being inside a shell
echoing big as an ego.
Your hair is heaven's water.
Your coming is a dawn made of all the air
I ever breathed. All movement seems
a mockery of stillness.
I know you try even harder than I
to hold off the darkness that's coming on,
the darkness that finishes off
the other half of me which you already are.

11

smell

Soft-pedalled tones from the spaced piano
keys of the clouds floating
off, and then streaming toward you from your face . . .
A memory cradled in the nasal passage
starts doubling in the brain,
as if a thought could be traced back
to its original odor—a corner
of linoleum in a summer house, or
the fragrance of a woman passing you in May,
the breeze lightly tracing her
like a pasture against your bare arm.

Remember how you thrilled her?—
It was her own world you described to her,
then took apart
to reveal its inner workings.
Your words were wild dogs
foaming up out of the turf, so full
they were of their own dimension.

She stands around you now,
the distance rolling off her in waves
that touch you like blotting paper
and spread through you like a shot.

12

some questions of distance

Who put our heads here?
Is your head near?
Is mine near yours?
Or are we ashes from a joint
blown into space
twisting to be somewhere else?
What if somewhere else were news
of here trying to clear the treetops? —
as if only what comes with strain
from far away is true or good . . .

Because you want it all,
we've heard of you.
Because you can't part with its memory,
we'll forget you.
Each morning, each evening,
and the blanks in-between,
I watch you belong to no one.

13

bits of thirst

You see I keep wanting to fly into
your country of constant affection
toward the white mountains of the west
where light isn't wasted on shadows
and snow does not bruise
against a fading door.
If all's downhill, then long peace
poisons the deepest wells,
and sleep is a rain pouring
on all our senses' chatter.

Balmy air, lowering daylight, something
of this evening not nailed down gently rises—
a forgotten knock headed in the direction of the stars that lay about
like bits of thirst you can see through
but not all the way to the other side.

14

the therapy of walking

Spring's foreglow in the cheeks of girls on the archery course,
the feathered arrow flush against the cheek-fuzz and tickling;
in the dirty mutt's spontaneously glowing member . . .

It makes me think of a rudder that has been steering the whole creaking
boatload out the open channel, suddenly visible, bigger than life.

If there must be flags, let them be pressed from our tongues,
waving hello and kissing goodbye to each other
in this flickering joust of affections and carnivorous appetites.

Until they are, you plunge into the streets
drawing and divvying up
                          the wild energy that abounds there,
and discover the therapy of walking—
the ingrown slugs whacked to a buoyancy
                          you admire in a woman's soaped body,
the first gift of intimacy brushing you
to the crest of the sexual wave that is your life.

15

august

In the long prehistory of August
it makes so little difference where
one looks for the sky, how far
from our nude and prickly skins the celestial
pie of space is nibbled, leaving
a planet of crusted rivers that flow
nowhere, empty as rooms
we carry in us.

What's clear is a father risen
at the head of the past with its peaked roof,
and all you can remember about falling asleep
stands in the doorway
in the form of a woman whose laughter invites
anything you might bring her
except your coming there alone.

16

poem

No longer awaiting my birth I leave
my quickening deaths behind me hoping
they will not follow through the dark
through my fear of the dark I step
awkwardly with my lit hoop of fire

Together we skip several rungs in the order of evolution
Ascension is the new order of the day
Birds swoop up to take a closer look at us
It is time the snow stopped falling on the flowers

On the beach which is also the sky
Each shadow waves its crutch at us

How can you be gone now
Always you have been nowhere but rhythmically under me
My hands your ears I whisper my unfinished secret to
While the cup of my voice dries in the sun

I love you for your daring not your constancy

Once we used nature like household utensils
Who will set up house with me

Could what you have called my silence be
The gathering of a new voice to sing you with

17

uprising in fall

The brown leaf of autumn in upright decline
strains to become the man it resembles.
Yet listen to the children of light
on the other side of the blue door
refusing to be born
just as you refuse to enter their darkness.

     You, who draw out
the blurring vapor trails of night and day,
who break off time
anywhere, like a loaf of bread—see
the wave leap high, singular in recoil!

Now it is right
that you are younger than your son,
older than your father;
that you laugh and welcome the October fly
streaking through the dank graves of the air
to mount itself, fly of topaz no womb hides from,
invisible thread
speckled with lightning, that bore you,
that bears you up,
while the nations do not survive morning,
wilt by noon, are buried at evening in the anthill.

her dream

For a long time after he left, I slept
and felt myself nothing but endless shore,
till in a blast of sea-fog rounding the headland,
I thought I saw his figure motioning me to follow.
His movements seemed slower, the young face older, set,
but my happiness was so great, more even
than when we were together and I used to playfully
balk when he urged me on, out past where either of us had gone.
Giving myself, I almost vanished,
but was carried back on a wind, violently shaken, a fallout of crystals.
Sunrise and sunset, I suffered the gradual abortion of longing;
the darkness hidden under the light;
sea-vapors without beginning or end, imperishable as my mother.

With the strength he had often used against me,
and a stubborn will I learned from him,
I gathered up the little remaining light stuck to my fingernails
and dreamed my desolation
into a horse so white, its smoothness reflected
the blue sky on its flank,
and I rode out to where I knew he was
gone, a storm in mid-ocean.

                                    In the center I found
a quietness so peaceful it left no desire
for praising it. Then I grew afraid he was not there,
that nothing could survive that stillness
where the water of time had turned into space.

                          I woke and saw
I had gone nowhere.
Ripples at my feet were only a breath
of that great hunger which is his power.

O if my nature is to be not fixed but flowing,
will he one day collect himself
into an eye,

19

and for once see this body opened and willingly emptied
to feed him, not bind his freedom?
Will he turn and look and tell me what I am?—
What I am to become?

20

the mine

The wheels are of quivering meat
The train is of oxygen
The tracks are of honey
The ore barely flickers
The cave-in is imminent
The light is severed
The sands are numerous
The entrance is a wind

21

poem for the left hand

You look the way I feel
inside my face
when no one's around.

22

almost dawn

Needles of starlight
    expanding out
and night licking
    the recent loss
      of a face
    deep down
inside you

23

the tides of her, the roots

(San Francisco)

Drenched in repose, the sky returns
hopeless with remembering   Smile
     jasmine candlesmoke   her sucking
lips body smooth as a dancefloor   as dark
     5 a.m. Castro Street's a cat's haunch   stretches
      and purrs the licked ears of lovers
      the furred paws descending dewy steps.

A swimmer thought lost, the sun
    crests a hilltop.   I'm sliding
      crosscountry
    on hips whittled into matchsticks
     to blaze a handful of Coney Island
    sand into a window
               big as California

the new

Two weeks out of San Francisco and it's
    Autumn   no dope   and trouble
                          in the frisky heart.
    Only thing new is autumn . . .
      How leaves shed and deepen
          as you shed, like that tree, and deepen,
as I drink,
    like the winter beast I am—all year.
It's for my empty veins I need your blood.
Watch my jaws open,
          the jaws of my ribcage.
    The bathroom faucet is running.
    It has been running quite awhile.
    A man is fixing it.
    Soon it will be quiet.
    I will miss the sound.
    The spirit runs on
               fevered dreaming.
Look!—in the sky, those batwings! . . . whose?

25

double libra

A mouth   a tongue   a throat
    lengthening
       the thin line of you
about to vanish,
    sometimes I would rather be an eye
       staring and silent
than this growling nerve
    sniffing your scent
       and the words you hold
over an inner track of longing
    lighting the way,
       because each day doubles
its likeness
    to your going
       down to the bottom of the sky.

the corroding air

At times, things close to sprouting
are called light   Warmth
        slows down to a mode of thinking.
Believe the river wasting away
            O roots, raise
                        the rat-sweating sky—
Revive the tasty
                pieces of nothing
        you left whirring in cider, in thighs.

        Here!—I give you the ripe fruit of enthusiasm
to slice thinner than a porcupine's
            stab, thinner than sound

the hot bullet

No one loves me like the hot
    bullet in my belly
Deep in thick reeds and radiant brass
    the odor of melted crayon
    the basement of a shoe
and you variously awake as a tribe
    your cry savage with promise
    plucks the sun's feathers
       bald on the block
Sky soft eggbox of jellyfish flopping
    over gunmetal Iowa pig
    blossoms a snowflake intricate
    as your eardrum   heavy or
    light as the weight of your pride
We are men   want a map of blossoms
    cheeky and soulful and rare
    and a savagery without forgiveness
      to keep alive the dog's
      the child's cry promising to bite
      hard as incest
Crickets making it in the grass you groomed
    and bedded down for them or any
    tangy whiff of ocean on the yellow plain
    loud loving with the intricate snoring
      of a tribe on its belly
What listening?—for the feathers of
    the eradicated city? a snowflake
    smuggled through summer in your flesh?
    or a ship flapping with burgeoning
    news toward some groggy stevedores
    unloading their eyes the color of television?
Energy without a face   milked at a sow's tit
    bottomless as a fire stepping
      out of her dress   melting
      her shape like soft crayons

Like lovers pollinated with the pain of distance
        theirs a misery blessed by stars collected
        in a frogpond on a balding plain
Moon, press your fingerprint on the crayoned
        city about to be eradicated—
Incest raining hard as nails bangs
        on a drumskin of newsprint
        bangs in the holds of ships
What are you doing to the savage in your belly, O men
        scavenging the dirty plain of a sow's tit!—
        while lovers are smuggling a yellow blossom
        through a snowstorm of television   no map
        no shoes   singing their bellies   the wells
        the sun's feathers soak up
At the bottom a fire the shape of a bull's horns
        waits for them—the space between horn tips
        is measured in stars and spurts of sow's milk
and so wakens the various radiances lovers keep alive
        and savage, the cheeky voyagers who cry
in the shape of jellyfish over a distance
                heavy as gunmetal
        with no witness but the ravenous cinders
                of their shoes hissing
                on the crayoned map   stretched
                and drumming on the block   the moon
                the melting wax of their bones

the friends

i

They have grown steadily
marked by an early disquiet
that has never left them, and deepened
by the need to be taken to heart
as doubt of what they had
believed would last is
on the increase.
              Some nights it pulls
their faces into lean strips
of licorice
        as they twist
along the curves of drifting highways
they will be remembered
as disappearing on.

ii

Scattering as far as things can go in a self-
propelled wind, they switch
lines, lovers and the inherited
compulsions they were fed on
and feed each other
as ambitions.
             Their ambitions have become
their faces. The holes they step into now
are in their heads.
              Each of their lives bears that much
more of the chaos the friends are
rich in.

iii

Last seen, they were giving themselves
up to a beauty as punishing as it lay wholly
outside their bodies: to enter
is to be swollen out of this world.

30

I sometimes think there is another life
without memory or confessions
kicking out of it.
               But if I had been told
that some day the sight of a room full of loved ones
could stir such an urge
for a getaway,

I wouldn't have believed it.

ode

As each cry not of celebration is a cry for help,
my own diminish. Home has grown
predictable as nostalgia.
But one must persist as if late for a Saturday night
date with a blonde goddess: as if our lapses from perfection
were cause for joy and parties
in which the ant-line of minutes walks
gracefully into a jar of honey, then out, beaming;
in which your body moving through sunlight sharpens,
a knife-edge through whalefat,
and some clown dressed like a crow escapes the rising
water with a strawberry in his beak—or
is that a rush of sperm caught in a drop of fire?
That the wings will give out is not a reason for despair.
Only that their freedom brings down something
like storms and minglings that seem endless, and then,
like the unfinished tale of your singleness
which never quite fit, disappear.

32

fractions

Morning light slides through the window
Sun oblique chutes a burial at sea

Cars on the causeway
Bugs full of wind

The white scaffolding erected with blocks of breath—
This is the coldness with no escape growing
Outward from the bone

Is the part of you that remembers the part
Of me that forgets?

Too much blood has been spilled
In every direction
To go on believing you can live
Only one way

Wind intent on becoming your ear

Stones, a marriage against all storms
In a garden you delight in
But cannot grow for yourself

The houses have no walls
The walls have no ears
If it were not for the cries you hear
How would you know
You were among the living?

When lovers waylay each other
What can we expect from enemies?

When will you no longer confuse
The loneliness that goes round and round
And the loneliness that goes forward—
The sweet words
And their savage odor?

Is it the deepness of the well that fascinates you
Or the well's face?

Great hole of space whistling through her grey eye

You do nothing   You are the done to

Between the eye and what it sees
Between the foot and the floor it reaches for
A ripping of ice at the pole or a scream of happiness
At how much is risked in coming this far
              to exist so briefly . . .
                    A match striking,
A spark amplified an entire day

It cuts the sharpest corners
It gets tired and leans against him

A curving inlet hollowed by sound, a handful of grain, sand
Now his purpose doesn't exceed his size

He and his friends, particles in a constellation of smoke
Drawing together for warmth

A foghorn forgets the tubing that shapes it and recalls
The frequency the wind inhabits

Vehemence: as in 'vehement as hell'

A typeface on white space
Less and less

Wind whistles a future between wooden teeth
The Ice Age at the window
Undevoured insect, grasping and refused

What is your whoosh? When it lessens, why does his
        heart contract?
Rumors rumors
More and more you's
Chopping it down

Each night stripping his ears of their rooms, he thanks
The stars there is something he cannot hold on to

Wind takes up what breathing left off

Listen to the mortared bricks singing
Their pulverized song, and his too,

In the attic of space
One inch from the top of his head.
In it are swallowed all celebrations and calls for help,
         all reasons for satisfaction.

Wind tongues your inner ear in the shape but not the color
Of wildflowers at terrific speed.
Growing unscrupulous as vegetation.

It neither promises nor threatens
It neither revives a mood nor points a direction
It knocks. You enter by listening where nothing divides
What holds and vibrates
From what falls away.

february

Your eyes float like sun grains
through their light, pollinating the air—
          If they graze and go, the same wind
that brought them, blows them away, the same hand.
Returning, they will appear as an orange
in the sky, the segments as windows, the focus sharper,
more acute. In them, I have seen more sky.

Back away, if that spark leaping from your throat
is not meant to catch fire to your hair;
if you don't mean to spread it each night
you move forward illuminated from within, like a spy.

You gather the blue of your eyes from jubilant swimmers
refreshed by their plunge, who step from the foam
onto the hills of this city, tidal waves
caught cresting in emery.

          Daily precipices egg you on
to faces so quietly sliced in half,
no one in the street feels a thing as they stand
the operation of atomic surgery
the minutes, like wiped blades,
perform not on flesh but something infinitely more
unmarriageable, slower, smoke.
                    Whatever stays indoors
is scarred by the reach of the animals born in cages;
whose claws grow sharper whether we feed them or not.

The emerald tree you stuck in the garden like a fishbone, blackens.
An ooze clear as lymph flows down the jewelled bark.
From a fork in the branches, a chill whips out
and brushes my face for the last time, ripping
off a piece to eat on the way.
                    It is a wound
I have never gotten used to, that holds me together. It can turn
a man into a killer.
I have wanted to move so deeply into you
not even the worms could touch me!

Dragging torn roots and creepers, spring
bites the blanks of clouds, drawing first blood.
The branches are made of light,
and the light branches out like a tongue wetting lips.
The grey paw lifts; I see
the hooked tapeworm that ate the light in your chest.

Farther out, the sea is whipping
green and black, turbulent and trite
as a mind too much in its body.
I see you hover on the crest of a white wave,
on an ocean smitten with amnesia.
The setting sun is half a woman
and half an odor melted down
from the plastic heat of electric clocks.
Can I fill your gaps with lightning—you,
who are growing beautiful, more beautiful than I am?

On the opposite hill, bits of foam
are houses, sparks caught glowing in a potter's cup.
As I approach, the windows are mirrors opening
on nothing if I did not picture your eyes
wiping the void with a washcloth.

Rooftops stagger, windows fall
inward without shattering glass. Birds, visible
motions of air, change partners in mid-flight,
and I know that you who were about to leave,
have lived another year in my body.

catching fire

Everywhere gutter musicians with rare saxophones
rise in the air like snowy egrets.

The night wolf drifts
on a coffin nailed with stars.

A man in an alley unravels
the feathers of a woman's body.

From the firmament above the rooftops
a hand rockets loose,
catching fire in the snow.

The one window, steam-laced with your breath,
splinters to moths,
the last white flutter of a brooding routine.
Heaven enough for one night.

By the jetty, a child rocks like a tide.
The moon is a bright town
risen from a hillside
leaving an emptiness in our lives
to either orbit or sink.

The child's cry nags the darkness into an orange
while I sit on a flight of stairs inside a bottle
and my heart rejoices over you, spilling out.
My desires are a crowd.
You are the best crowd-pleaser in sight.
The best landscape is you on your back.
The prettiest flowers, your legs in the air.

dago

From flat dry midlands, a crab of the air
  zigzagged to shore.
There I could not turn my heart
  into a girl,
 though the hand I touched you with was a nerve-
  end of my balls.
   Booming surf
  through its sound barrier opens
   to a friend who said:
    'You see too much.'
I wanted to curl the rest of the night
  in the spark that fell from her eye.
Now by this ocean, I wake holding less of memory
  and more of this morning's freshness,
  honed waves crested
   with new space, sky at your feet,
    light of the desert,
  where to open a door
   is to have all the winds
    rush through you like a house.
I want to walk forever
    the slopes of your body
    on my hands,
  you who taste of mothers
    in all this trafficked meat.

1972: year of the rat

From the east where you lay
emerges a black sky like a model
of a new car.
I awoke before dawn.
A year has fallen into a leaf.
The leaf looks wiser for it, dry as an Indian
about to be blown off the prairie.
The moon has disappeared, another beauty
walked all over.
At such a time, the walls speak
of whom we have eaten with,
and you hear through a glass skull
like a tree pelted with asteroids,
while a small motor burns
the fatty tissue of the state
and the plum-ripe slum
at its core.
There is a place in the maple grove
that grows fresher with use.
Bring your eye, your third eye,
the sex of all that is visible,
and the fattened pig of innocence.

41

for mandelstam

I had wanted to stop
and listen closely to the words
thoughtlessly leading my days
all through the same needle;
why what I blessed in the morning,
by evening, turned back and judged me. . . .

The words we say and the words we don't say . . .
It feels good to talk to you,
though I'm not sure you were meant for listening.
But I have forgotten what I wanted to say,
and a thought floats in the shadows
where it speaks to other thoughts, about nothing.

In the muslin dark, in the velvet breathing dark,
the eyes of loved women flare
like clouds the sun sets in.
Let me be in their service
like the others mumbling
inane and blessed words without meaning,
not for the Word
but the cherry-bitten look it draws from you.

In the days rolling by like barrels
from some maniac's hand,
I have forgotten what I have judged,
I have forgotten what has judged me,
I'm not even jealous anymore;
I'm waving to you.

everywhere's face

Her smile or frown is all the space you see around.
Give her time, she'll reveal
the little about less which you call everything
if only you don't ask.
Wisdom bores her, but may excite you.
Her attention lies in leaving the dreaming
                              up to you,
the one in which fucking her is like halving the sun.
She may have no dreams, except
for those of you sloshing through the traffic and the rain toward the job,
and that's real,
              like loss is real,
as sometimes in despondency we flash on
only what we're not, or were, and not yet on what
we're dying to be.

              Then she goes out or comes in. Then
you find yourself
taking on more than you can handle. Fiery
comets madly whizzing in the stratosphere are more predictable.
Of all revolutions spoiled by slush of feeling, this
is the slushiest. It is a bucket
into which night and day have fallen. It is no fun.
In winter, when the weather goes down,
you had better come closer to hear her singing.
To miss it is ice;
To hear it is fire you want to take apart
and put together in wondrous ways that keep her close, warm,
                              daft and moaning.

in the running

The highest window has melted into the sky
and the women, looking up, have become
whatever they were so intently gazing at.
Heaven, still too blue to be kissed, is wiped clean
as something in you feels the sublime
kick of what will surpass you. Welcome it.
Surprise. You have just discovered the true
purpose of your arms and eyes.
If what you see in the wind turns
out to be a man wearing a stocking over his face,
don't be alarmed. His teeth are feathers
searching for a twig of sunlight
in your throat.
                    Then you run
into her. Then you hear wings
in the center of bone beating a passage
too wide and deep for you
not to crave.
                    Marvelous then
to treat each other's body like a soul
about to take on a grandeur
for being so fearless, fragile and more
than ourselves.

44

autumn

I've let all the members of my household go
their separate ways.
All those closest to me are out of reach.
Everything—in the heart, on the earth—
is filled with the emptiness it always was.

Now I'm with you here in the prospector's cabin.
The woods are empty of people, perhaps of animals.
When an old flame dies,
smoke gets in your eyes.

We're the only ones now
for the logs in the wall to stare at.
We never promised to storm barricades.
We'll go to hell with eyes open.

At one, we'll take our seats; at three, we'll leave—
I, with a book, you with your sewing.
When dawn breaks we won't notice
what time we finished kissing.

Make a stir, leaves, as you flutter down—
more colorfully, with more daring!
And raise the level of yesterday's bitterness
in the cup by adding today's thirst.

Craving, possessiveness, the worship of beauty . . .
Let's scatter like smoke in these September oats.
Dear heart, bury yourself in this downpour;
let go, go mad.

You undress with as much abandon
as this grove sheds its leaves,
when you fall into my arms
in your gown with its silken tassles.

47

You are the miracle on the march that finishes,
when living sickens more than sickness does.
The root of beauty is daring,
and that's what draws us together.

—adapted from Pasternak.

48

the sixth sense

How fine is the wine that loves us,
and the wholesome bread offering itself
to the oven for our sake,
and the woman who allows us to love her
after she's tried us to her heart's full.

But what are we to make
of a pumpkin sunset
over a sky that's growing colder, more silent
and more terribly calm?
What are we to make of deathless poems . . . ?

You can't eat, or drink, or kiss them . . .
The moment flies apart
though we wring it in our hands,
and parts of ourselves pass
each other, like strangers, without nodding.

Like a boy, distracted from his games, stares
at the bathing girls,
and though knowing nothing of love—
like a waterdrop sizzling on hot metal—
he boils on a pinpoint of desire;

just as in earliest mud-time
the slimey amphibian, feeling
under its hide the aching back-buds
of wings teething skyward,
squealed with impotence, caught in thickets,

so, age after age—how long, O Lord?—
under the revolving knives of nature and art
our spirit cries out,

49

the flesh shrivels,
as they sweat to bring an organ
of the sixth sense to birth.

—adapted from the Russian of Nikolai Gumilev.

50

mediterranean

Ancient one, I am drunk on the voices
that swell from your mouths swinging
like green bells when they open,
peel back and fall away.
My house, those distant summers,
and you, were neighbors, remember
there the sun baked one's daydreams
to black bread, and mosquito whirlwinds
plugged the air, letting nothing through.
Stunned today as then, near you
I no longer feel myself worth
the solemn warning of your breath.
You taught me first
that the small ferment
of my heart was nothing but a moment
of yours: that at bottom I kept
your risky law: to be vast and various
yet fixed: to rid myself of waste
as you do, throwing on the shores
among cork algae starfish
the useless trash that pollutes your deep

—Montale

51

don't ask

Don't ask here for the word that squares off
our shapeless breath, nor the letters of fire
that announce it and blaze like a crocus
lost in the middle of a dusty field.

Ah, the man who strides with confidence,
a friend to others and to himself,
and doesn't care that the dog-days stamp
his shadow on a crumbling wall.

Don't ask for the formula to open worlds.
A few dry thorny syllables want
to tell you only this,
what we are *not,* what we do *not* want.

—Montale

52

on a letter not written

Is it for a swarming of daybreaks, for a few
threads on which the raw
fleece of life snags and is strung
into hours and years, that the dolphins in pairs
are playing today with their young? Oh to hear
nothing of you, to escape the beam
of your gaze. It's far different on earth.

I cannot vanish nor reappear; night's
reddening furnace is late,
evening drags out;
prayer is torture and not yet
among the jutting rocks has there reached you
the bottle from the sea. The empty
wave breaks on the point, at Land's End.

—Montale

53

tramontana

Now rippling anxieties race out
their last circle on the lake,
and the vast sizzling everywhere—
tree-rot, slag-heap, beehive—drifts down, fades.
Today one iron will's whip snaps
overhead, uproots the bushes, breaks
the palm-leaf's back and in the stone-hard sea
carves deep channels crested with foam.
Rock blubbers to clay, clay boils to lava,
the mind's rough diamond turns to jelly,
and nature, a bowl of batter, is whipped to butter.
A long towering cry jets skyward
and I cannot tell if what I see
is a bird or spirit tapering to bird.
And you who draw your arms in
like a flower that turns its back on the sun,
how afraid you are of those lawless flocks
that crowd more and more soul-space out of existence.
Today, frail life, sirrocoed in mid-air,
hold on tight to these few roots, this earth.

—Montale

54

sea-front

The shore-breeze rises, tearing
the dark to bits of carbon,
and the shadow you throw on the fragile
plaza wall blisters. Too late

to be yourself! Down from the palm
jumps the rat and the lightning-
gods, like children grown tired of the rules,
play with matches near the gas.

The eyelash you lift in surprise
is lit like a fuse.

—Montale

55

from the blind woman

adapted from Rilke

Stranger:
   I've come here from across the sea.
Woman:
   What? To this island? . . . Here?
Stranger:
   I'm still in the boat.
   I've brought it alongside you, gently.
   It moves with the tide.
   Its flag blows landward.
Woman:
   I'm an island. Alone.
   And rich.
   I loved my eyes when the grooves were still clean.
   Then my nerves hollowed out
   from so much use.
   At first, I bled tears,
   my heart emptied; where to?—I didn't know.
   One day I found them, though,
   all my feelings, all I amount to,
   all crowding and crying
   at my walled-up eyes that didn't flinch.
   They may have been standing there year after year.
   Those days are still with me
   when they appeared so washed-out
   they didn't recognize anything here.
   The path to my eyes was overgrown.
   I've forgotten how, or when.
   Now things inside me move around,
   sure-footed, carefree, emotions amble
   like convalescents enjoying their daily walk
   inside my body's greenhouse, round and round.

Some, stooping, pore over
flowers they planted long ago;
the younger, restless ones, stare out.
When one of them approaches my edge
I turn transparent window.
My foot learns something new about the stones
it touches; can talk with those it stirs.
Out of the dovecote of daybreak
my voice rises with the wingbeat of each bird.
There's nothing I lack;
all colors are rendered back
as sound and fragrance.
What's a book to me?
There are no bounds to what I see.
Leaves of trees are being scrolled by the air.
I know what the words to prayers are,
and sometimes, whispering, repeat them.
And Death, who snaps eyes like flower stalks,
won't find me where he walks . . .

Stranger:
    I know.

the demon's speech to tamarra

from Lermontov's *The Demon*

I swear by the first day of Creation
I swear by the last

I swear by the wretchedness of evil
      by the preciousness of good

I swear by the bitter fruit of the Fall
      by the bloody dream of victory

I swear by my first sight of you
      and our imminent parting

I swear by the fawning parasites
      my fate has tied to me

I swear by the swords of envious angels
      my abiding enemies

I swear by Heaven which is my Hell

I swear by your first glance
      by your first tear
      by the palest breath from your lips
        the lightest touch of your hair

I have renounced my ancient vengence
I have given up my pride

From now on the poison of my temptations
      no longer will inflame the lusts of men
I want to make my peace with them

I want to love and pray
I want to believe in goodness

With my tears I want to wash
      the scars of celestial fire from my brow
      now worthy of you

Oh believe me
I'll let the world go
        in blissful ignorance without me
        to live its eternal life

        if only
        you'll love me

floats

Gray now
Now tell him that
Tell that
And I one when empty
Tell him on
The will winding unheard   and leaving
When there consider his courts
His seas his cows
And join the echo that tells
Tell him that
Tell him we are the alone along in herds
With nothing among us in passing
As some see with that nothing

And in they take a smaller they
As though they were distances
Of themselves to us
And all having is wild smelling

61

You came to and O
With grief
At looking
And all is it
Leaving and watching from today
And tomorrow
Before any blackness the what
My what
I cannot do
I have halved I
But will look even when there
Believe there is still
Go in the gold waking me

62

All animals myself
I with remembering
What among the wheels
We are   we eat   we are you
I did the wheels say
There we lay
And you it calls
Know you   I know
Every like a long time ago
Something I was

Ages

Now one thing can stop
Not you
Once you go   you go on
What
What
No what

Who

It is the go on doing
It is the do on the way

It is the dew

64

You live for the every
O the every brim
The every you can hear in all
And before that   during away
It had a hand in the dent we wore
It had care   it had source
And went the distance

65

Came the
Came the
Came the
Eyes
Cheers
And were kept

66

Inside the crawl
Hollow and how
Some
Some held birds wheeling past
Some hugged their soot
Saw nothing
Crying near in a jug   no one
Wondering which offering today
The hand all may almost lie
Knowing the light was heavy
And why

It had from over the white grown
They felt   their roots
And nowhere asking where
When April sinks
Days with no you that you know
And now is always now what?
The sky multiply
Not the you you hear
But the not that is real
In you
The not you multiply

Sometimes almost I am
Can try one
At times struck still
Sometimes even I open
On all sides

If I could try the world like creatures can
And not forget
It must be all different
And more

The turning in your tone, so
Cars smell cool
Much neon gas everything
These lids
And the air apart
Where so many roads part
You from me
But don't look it

Or is
Or is
Finally
Living your voice in the air

It is the thee bird
Thinking in a warble
And little lurk primates
Nicely quivered
Humming direction

And you I will tell of it
Is it you? Not yet
It rises
It goes
It follows
It falls not to you
Moving on with nothing of hours

The lights that were
Together under that gathering
By and by

71

The sun friends us
It goes from time to time
Containing everyone
The old birds   the beasts in hinges
Where cities eat their shadows
Without moving

Strange to finish off
To one side
Without a head
  What part?
  What able?
  What coat?
  What neck?
  What yours?

  Whose head?

All the centuries cleanly far don't take

You rise
You give
You take
You grow
You bear up
You vanish on

    All new

When you show
The clock has no place
You being
Whoever else is me.

hold, open, look

The waiting tracks of gone birds
raise their hands.
I have no wheels, am no stationwagon,
cannot carry your sweat on my back,
nor unroll what I mean
into a sleeping bag.
In grass the color of clouds

hangs the junk of speeding
fame: a slug limed on a brick.
And next to it, speech, the thinnest muscle
having to lift weights.
Fine as an eye of honey
in the daily swill,
we took it for hunger,
we took it for meat.
Now it comes chewing, billowy lion head
of fog tossing over the hill, chewing
itself shapeless—lips, nose, feet.

Who is that angel in white sneakers
you saw arriving on the playing fields of paradise?
Not me.
Each of us is many
infants made from the holes of sponges.
O be buttoned safely
        into that soaked home's porous drift . . .
Like a root-hand in a new skin,
hold, open, look.

75

the gardener's note, cliffside, pt. loma

Will the sun show today?
Will the water darken or clear
in which a naked woman bends, smoothing
the surface with the flat of her hands?
From this height, she is no one I know,
though she could be the pregnant woman
who took acid on the beach
and lay down to have her child
as the tide came in.

From here, she is more exposed
than juice under the bruised skin of ripe fruit;
her face, an orange in the mist,
innocent of how in peril it hangs from the branch.
How can you tell her how many other worlds
smelling of torn roots and rain also gather
in what you feel for her?
She trusts her fragileness to the ocean
as if sand were the tiles of her bathroom.

I want to be near a whore
the first morning she feels the last bloom go
dead in her bones, and sighs.
I want to hear it,
like the music of bridges to a drowning man.
Funny, how when things fall apart,
a humming light cuts through . . .
How a bus drive giving directions through his fat,
an old woman's face rising out of its wrinkles
to shape a smile,
seem heroic.

After days of not speaking,
you wonder if the silence isn't the last beginning left;

if the freshness that stings
wasn't in your safe-keeping . . .
I think it's time I learned
from whatever in the air or on the earth
will survive our kind.
Maybe, when I return, things will be changed,
and I'll stay.

77